SHY SOPHIE

igloo

Sophie was terribly shy. When Aunty Pat and Uncle Kevin came to visit, she would hide behind the comfy chair. If the postman called with a package, she would run upstairs.

One day at the supermarket, Sophie and her mum met Mr Franks, Sophie's music teacher. "Hello Sophie," he said.

"Hello," smiled Sophie's mum, as Sophie pulled the furry hood of her coat right down over her face, "She's shy, you know!"

Mr Franks nodded, understandingly.

Sophie's birthday party was a bit of a problem! All her friends came to the house and brought her lots of presents but Sophie hid under the table.

"What's the matter?" asked her mum.

"She's shy, you know," said Nancy, her best friend. "She doesn't want us to sing 'Happy Birthday' to her."

Sophie's mum was pleased that her friends understood but she wished that Sophie would join in all the fun.

At school one day, Mr Franks announced a special talent show.

The children were very excited and spent ages deciding what to do. Nancy would read poetry. Timmy wanted to tell jokes. Dave really, really wanted to walk the tightrope, but Mr Franks said it was too dangerous. Sydney just wore his underpants on his head!

Sophie looked at the floor and was as quiet as a mouse. "What about you, Sophie?" said Mr Franks. "What would you like to do?"

But Sophie couldn't speak; she was just too shy.

Clarissa went over to Sophie.

"Don't be shy, Sophie," she said. "Everybody's good at something." Sophie just shook her head. "Yes, you are," said Clarissa.

"Besides, how do you know if you don't try in the first place? I never knew that I could play the recorder, until I tried." Clarissa pulled her recorder out of her bag. "Now watch me," she said, and she put the recorder to her lips and played the most beautiful tune.

"That's right," said Simon. "Watch me," and he took a run and a jump and did the most perfect cartwheel at the front of the classroom.

Everybody clapped and cheered. "I had no idea that I could do gymnastics, until I tried."

Sophie was smiling. She had dreamed lots and lots of times of being a singer on a stage but she was far too shy to sing.

She reached up to whisper in Clarissa's ear.

"What's that?" said Clarissa, "you want to sing, but you're too shy?"

Sophie nodded quickly and looked at the floor.

"Well," said Mr Franks, thinking quickly, "this calls for a sing-along. Now everybody, let's get together around the piano and sing a favourite tune. Sophie, I want you to stand right at the back, where nobody can see you. Perhaps Clarissa will stand next to you."

Mr Franks began to play the piano. All the children stood round and sang. Sophie had moved right to the back with Clarissa and Clarissa started to sing along.

Sophie looked around. Nobody seemed to be taking any notice of her. They were far too busy enjoying themselves. When it came to the second chorus, Sophie plucked up courage and joined in.

The music continued and Sophie sang along, smiling happily. She was enjoying herself so much, she didn't notice that the rest of the class had stopped singing.

They just stood and listened in amazement. "What a beautiful voice you have," said Mr. Franks when the song was over.

All the children clapped loudly. Sophie blushed. "I never knew that singing could make you feel so good," she said.

The day of the talent show arrived. Sophie stood all alone on the stage in front of hundreds of people. There was even a photographer there from the local newspaper.

The music started and Sophie sang a lovely song.

No one was at all surprised when she won. Apart from Sophie, that is.

"I'm not going to be shy any more," she announced.

The following day, there was a picture of the winner of the contest on the front page of the newspaper.

also available...

Rude Roger   Dirty Dermot   Pickin' Peter   Space Alien Spike   Silly Sydney   Nude Nigel

Shy Sophie   Cute Candy   Royal Rebecca   Grown-up Gabby   Terrible Twins   Show-off Sharon